GW00385203

49 Excuses for Not Tidying Your Bedroom

Published by Curious Squirrel Press

Book cover design by: James Warwood
Book interior design by: Mala Letra / Lic. Sara F. Salomon

ISBN: 9798411562446
ebook ISBN: B0OGV9V87S

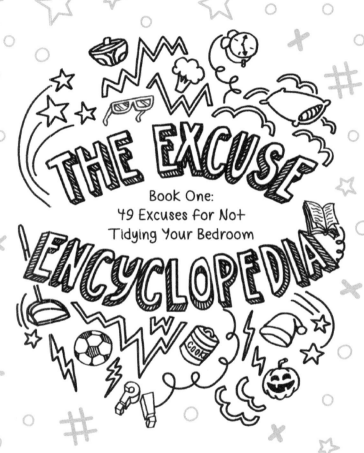

THE EXCUSE

Book One:
49 Excuses for Not
Tidying Your Bedroom

ENCYCLOPEDIA

James Warwood

BOOK ONE

49 Excuses for Not Tidying Your Bedroom

BEDROOM EXCUSES

1. THE (MAKE-BELIEVE) FRIENDS EXCUSE

My imaginary friends are tidying my room as we speak . . .

. . . Laura is dusting. Boris is tidying up. Jenny is searching for my other green sock. Ronald is hoovering, but you can't hear him because he's using an invisible hoover.

2. THE INFECTIOUS EXCUSE

I've got Multi-Coloured Chicken Pox!

. . .

. . . my body is covered in red, green, blue and orange spots. It says on this felt tip pen that multi-coloured chicken pox is highly contagious and that the infected child should rest until the spots fade away. As these are new felt tip pens I suspect I'm going to be ill for a long time.

3. THE ACTIVIST EXCUSE

I'm on a Tidiness Strike. So far I haven't lifted a finger for 8 days, 15 hours and 47 seconds . . .

. . . well someone's got to speak up for Caterpillar Rights.

4. THE MASTERPIECE EXCUSE

I've become a Contemporary Modern Artist. This is my latest work, I call it 'The Untidy Room of a Young Genius' . . .

. . . I reckon some French millionaire should arrive any minute now to buy my masterpiece. So don't touch ANYTHING!!!

5. THE UPSET STOMACH EXCUSE

I can't tidy my room because I've got butterflies in my stomach . . .

. . . I should never have eaten that Caterpillar Sandwich for lunch!

6. THE OVER-
PHOBIC EXCUSE

Help!

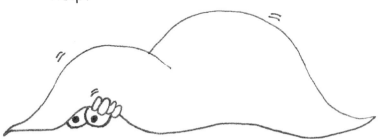

. . . There's a spider[1] under my bed. It's teasing me because I'm too scared to play Scrabble[2], Go Fish[3], Snap[4], , Twister[5], Hungry Hippos[6], Battleships[7], and Guess Who[8][9][10] and then it called me Floccinaucinihilipilification.[11]

---

1 Arachnophobia - fear of spiders.

2 Verbophobia - fear of words.

3 Ichthyophobia - fear of fish.

4 Ligyrophobia - fear of loud noises.

5 Chromatophobia - fear of colours.

6 Phagophobia - fear of swallowing or of eating or of being eaten.

7 Arithmophobia - fear of numbers.

8 Peladophobia - fear of bald people.

9 Pogonophobia - fear of beards.

10 Xenophobia - fear of strangers or foreigners.

11 Hippopotomonstrosesquipedaliophobia - fear of long words (and hippos).

7. THE SPIRITUAL EXCUSE

Thanks to meditation I've discovered my deeply spiritual inner self that doesn't require a tidy bedroom to experience lasting happiness and inner peace . . .

. . . you look stressed, maybe you should try it too.

8. THE REVISION EXCUSE

Sorry but I'm revising for my spelling test tomorrow . . .

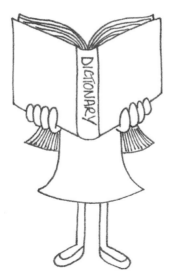

. . . I know it's only a 10 word test, but Miss Print said there will be a surprise bonus word. So I decided to be thorough and learn all 60,000 words in the English Dictionary.

9. THE NEW BUSINESS EXCUSE

Welcome to my new business venture. I call it . . .

. . . I'd be happy to mess up your bedroom as well, for a small fee.

10. THE IMPORTANT RESEARCH EXCUSE

Aaaaaaaargh! You made me lose count! . . .

. . . I am doing some very important research for AbsolutelyPointlessFacts. com, counting how many toes a centipede has. Now I'll have to start all over again. 1, 2, 3 . . .

11. PROFESSIONAL DEVELOPMENT EXCUSE

A career advisor visited our school yesterday and told us to start practicing what we want to be when we grow up . . .

. . . so I'm practicing being unemployed. I'm already very good at sleeping in past lunch time and I've mastered not tidying my bedroom, so next on my professional development list is to watch TV all day and shout at the neighbour's cat.

12. THE PARENT-CHILD-SWITCH-A-ROO EXCUSE

Have the court papers not arrived yet? I've adopted you . . .

. . . so go tidy your room! And lights out at 8:30pm

13. THE ZOMBIE INVASION EXCUSE

Don't panic. Zombies have taken over the entire town, surrounded the house and are about to . . . SMASH!!!

. . . they've broken in! Quickly lock yourselves in the basement. I'll fight them off with the inflatable baseball bat I won at the Carnival.

14. THE PLAGUE OF QUESTION MARKS EXCUSE

These question marks are refusing to leave until I've solved the greatest mystery in the known universe: 'The Meaning of Life' . . .

. . . this could take 8-10 years so tidying my bedroom will have to wait.

15. THE FAR-TOO-BUSY EXCUSE

I can't tidy my room, my schedule is jam-packed . . .

. . . I've got a board meeting at 9am, a multi-million project to plan and a mountain of emails to reply to. You'll have to speak with my secretary, Mrs Potato Head, she'll pencil it into my diary early next week.

16. THE SCIENTIFIC EXCUSE

Did you know that a recent scientific study has shown that 92% of children who never tidied their rooms achieved better grades in schools, grew up to become the worlds most successful and happy people . . .

. . . If you don't believe me then email the scientist. His name is Dr Google.

17. THE NATURE LOVER EXCUSE

I just received a letter from the Government declaring that my bedroom has become a Protected Nature Reserve for several species of endangered bacteria . . .

. . . so if I tidy my room I'll be breaking the law. You've always taught me to live within the law of this great nation, so for the protection of these microscopic germs I promise to never tidy my bedroom ever again.

18. THE CLEVER NEW WORD EXCUSE

I learnt a new word at school this week, 'delegation' . . .

. . . now I shall explain what it means with a demonstration. Dad, fold up my clothes. Mum, pick up all my Lego. When you're finished come back to me for another demonstration.

19. THE RECORD BREAKER EXCUSE

Harry is currently attempting the World Record for the longest whistle . . .

. . . DO NOT DISTURB!!!

20. THE TACTICAL TANTRUM EXCUSE

You should be warned . . .

. . . I've finished my tactical tantrum course, graduated top of my class and received my degree in 'Getting What I Want All The Time.'

21. THE RICH KID EXCUSE

I've given up being a little kid to become a handsome billionaire . . .

. . . so one of my many servants will tidy my room shortly and give you a complimentary back massage for your inconvenience.

22. THE MOST POWERFUL WIZARD EXCUSE

Be quiet Muggles! I've found the Elder Wand and fixed it with Sellotape from the kitchen drawer. I am now the most powerful wizard in the world . . .

. . . what's the spell to make it rain Chocolate Frogs?

23. TREAT YOUR PARENTS TO A HOLIDAY EXCUSE

I know you're both very stressed from raising a lazy son, so I've booked us an all-expenses paid holiday to Disney Land . . .

. . . don't worry about the money. I used your credit card.

24. THE EVIL TWIN EXCUSE

I'm your daughter's evil twin sister . . .

. . . I've come to sabotage her tidy reputation. Now if you would excuse me all this sabotaging has made me peckish. Which way to the fridge?

25. THE ALLERGIES EXCUSE

I've had a severe allergic reaction to clean air, so please don't tidy my room. It's the only thing keeping me alive! . . .

. . . I would lift my bedding to show you the grotesque rash across my body but I've also recently discovered that I'm allergic to lifting as well.

26. THE FAKE DOCUMENTARY EXCUSE

I hope you don't mind but I've signed our family up to be on a documentary. It's called 'The Strictest Parents on the Planet and their Long-Suffering Children' . . .

. . . this is Steve the camera man, he'll be recording everything you do and say 24 hours a day 7 days a week. Well don't be rude, say hello.

27. THE MILITARY COUP EXCUSE

While you have been busying yourselves with everyday life I have been raising an army, a Bathroom Army. I DECLARE WAR! . . .

. . . Octopus of Terror, capture my spotty sister's room. Rubber Ducky Regiment, lay siege to the kitchen then sweep through the downstairs kingdoms. I shall lead the Toothbrush Squadron and the Bleach Cannons to the Throne Room and take this Household as mine.

28. THE GHOSTLY EXCUSE

Whoooooooooo. Whooooooooooooo. Whoooooooooooooooooooooooo. I am the Ghost of Christmas Present . . .

. . . What? It isn't Christmas yet? Oh, my mistake, I'll be going then. Be sure to save me some turkey and a Christmas Cracker on my return.

29. THE AMATEUR ASTRONAUT EXCUSE

How can I tidy my room when my head is full of curiosity? I'm tired of the theories. I'm sick of the rumours. I need to know . . .

. . . is the moon made of cheese? It will be the most important scientific breakthrough since the 'Heated Toilet Seat'. If I'm not back in time for dinner, leave me some in the microwave please.

30. THE TEAMWORK EXCUSE

My teacher told me to practice working as a team . . .

. thirty imaginary cacti

. . . Mum, pick up all my dirty washing and then take my dirty cups to the kitchen. Dad, tidy my bed and then hoover the carpet. I'll water my imaginary Cactus with my imaginary Watering Can until you're done.

31. THE EVE OF HIBERNATION EXCUSE

It'll have to wait till next year because winter is fast approaching. It's time to hang up my work boots and hibernate . . .

. . . didn't you know I'm part-human, part-squirrel. Wake me up when American Idol is back on.

32. THE RELIGIOUS CONVERT EXCUSE

I've been converted to Crispyanity . . .

. . . my religion commands me to follow the 'Crisps, Crisps & More Crisps' diet, to never tidy my room, to stand up and salute every crisp TV advert and collect empty crisps packets as offerings to the Potato God.

33. THE ADVICE FROM MY THERAPIST EXCUSE

The therapist you hired to cure my Compulsive Lying Disorder thinks I need a holiday in Hawaii to learn how to surf and become a limbo champion . . .

. . . she also thinks you should pay.

34. THE CHANGE OF CAREER EXCUSE

You always call me a cheeky monkey so I finally took your advice and became the Monk who looks after all the keys to the Monastery . . .

. . . you should see my bedroom in the monastery, it's spotless! Plus if I'm invited to a Star Wars themed Birthday Party I only need the ears and I could go as Yoda.

35. THE UNDER-PAR PARENTING EXCUSE

Rule 179 in 'The Good Parenting Guide' clearly states "when telling your daughter to go and clean her bedroom you must place your left hand on your hip, point to the bedroom with our righthand, and shoot lasers through your eyes burning two holes in her soul" . . .

. . . now go upstairs, learn this guide off-by-heart and practice, practice, practice. I'll be in my messy bedroom when you're ready.

36. THE RIDDLER EXCUSE

Ok I'll tidy my room, but first a riddle . . .

. . . the beginning of eternity, the end of time and space, the beginning of every end, and the end of every place. What am I? . . .

. . . THE LETTER 'E'.

37. THE PLAYGROUND EXCUSE

I would tidy my room but I'm stuck in the mud . . .

. . . someone tagged me just as I was leaving school and I had to waddle home like this!

38. THE TEACHERS ADVICE EXCUSE

My teacher told me I should take a long hard look at myself . . .

. . . I decided to start from my shoes and work up. So far I'm up to my belt buckle which means this homework should take another hour or two.

39. THE PRANKSTER EXCUSE

Please, sit down. I have an important announcement to make . . .

. . . FAAAAAAAART! I put Woppie Cushions on your chairs. Hehehe.

40. THE ALMOST WORLD CHAMPION EXCUSE

But I can't tidy my room! Look at this . . .

. . . I'm 4th in the Angry Birds World Rankings, just 7 points away from being the best bird flinger in the entire world! So I think you'll agree this is far more important than something as trivial as 'tidying'.

41. THE SUPERHERO EXPERIMENT EXCUSE

I've been spending all my time genetically mutating this centipede, then I've been leaving it's cage open and pretending to take a photo of this cardboard cut-out of Mary Jane . . .

. . . just imagine having 100 arms and legs! I could tidy my room, play computer games and update my Facebook status all at the same time.

42. THE SECRET AGENT EXCUSE

Just got a call from MI6. James Bond is on his holidays so they've asked me to be his replacement . . .

. . . by the way this phone is due to self-destruct in 5 seconds. Would you put it in the outside bin for me as I've got to go and save the world!

43. THE ROCK STAR EXCUSE

Haven't you heard the big news? My band - 'The Teddy Bears' - just signed a record deal after head lining at the Church Annual Picnic . . .

. . . so I figured a bunch of screaming fans will storm into my room any second now, looking for anything they can take home to make a shrine in their bedrooms.

44. PARENT-CHILD PEACE AGREEMENT EXCUSE

I think you'll find I cleaned my bedroom in March this year . . .

. . . It's only October now and as you well know the Child-Parent Peace Agreement of 2011 clearly states 'children only have to clean their bedrooms once a year'. Don't make me call the UN.

45. THE PPP EXCUSE

The PPP (Pushy Parents Police) just called and threatened to throw you guys in prison for 'Repeated-Harassment, Kissing in Public & Wearing Odd Socks Outside the House' . . .

. . . but don't panic, I told them you were taking me to the beach for ice cream today so you're off the hook. But be warned, next time I won't be so lenient!

46. THE LOST BOY EXCUSE

I've been in Neverland for the past 6 months and the first thing you say is 'tidy your room' . . .

. . . haven't you missed me? I used up all my fairy dust from Tinkerbell to come home! Where's my hug!?

47. THE ROCK & ROLL EXCUSE

Have you heard of the drummer from 'The Who' (a band from the 1960's your parents would have loved) He's called Keith Moon? . . .

. . . apparently he once drove a Bentley into a swimming pool and he trashed every hotel room he ever stayed in! So I imagine that compared to Mr Moon's bedroom, mine is extremely tidy. While we're on the subject could we convert the garden into a swimming pool and convert my sister's room into my new drumming room?

48. THE FORCE-FIELD EXCUSE

Really . . . well I've forged an invisible anti-adult force-field around my entire bedroom . . .

. . . if you try to step in here you'll immediately turn into a pile of dust! Go ahead, step into my room and see if I'm bluffing.

49. THE RITE OF PASSAGE EXCUSE

Look, I get it. Tidying my bedroom is a rite of passage that all children must go through . . .

. . . Your parents told you to tidy your bedroom and their parents told them to tidy their bedroom and on and on it continues. This will teach me the importance of responsibility and cleanliness and integrity that I will carry with me into adulthood (and then one day I will have sweet revenge on my children by telling them to tidy their bedrooms). So, I'll do it, as long as you wipe that smile off your face and give me a hand.

BONUS: NEW YOGA POSITION EXCUSE

Can't you tell? . . .

Yoga Position: 'the Lazy Slop'

. . . I'm in the middle of a yoga session. In fact, I'm so good I've invented my own yoga position (and mastered it). Tidying my room will ruin the inner tranquillity I've been working so hard to strengthen, plus the Teenage Mutant Ninja Turtles is on.

BONUS: SPOT EXCUSE

I can't tidy my bedroom . . .

. . . Why? Because if I move from this spot the world will end! So, I'm going to need you to get me a can of coke with a big straw and angle the TV towards me. The entire population of the world thanks you.

BONUS: STARFISH EXCUSE

I've been trying to tidying my bedroom all day . . .

. . . But I've lost my sight, smell, taste and hearing due to a freak fishing accident.

BONUS: FLOORDROBE EXCUSE

Welcome to my 'Floordrobe' . . .

New Sock Drawer

DANGER ZONE
(school clothes)

Laundry
Pile

New
Underpants
Draw

. . . I know what you're thinking. It looks like I haven't tidied my room. But I can assure you that although it may look like a mess, it's actually a well organised mess.

BONUS: MISSING SOCK EXCUSE

Bedroom tidying has had to be paused . . .

. . . I've lost a sock! My current working theory is that my missing sock, the old TV remote and dad's shed key have banded together and fled to Mexico to start a new life together.

BONUS: MOORDEB EXCUSE

Did you know that bedroom spelt backwards is . . .

. . . Which in Dutch roughly translates to 'a child's sacred sanctuary void of all adult influence'. So, that's why I can't tidy my bedroom.

BONUS: HOLEY EXCUSE

Put my sock in the bin? No way . . .

. . . This sock is holey. It must be preserved for future generations.

BONUS: YUMMA YUM BIRD EXCUSE

I can't tidy my bedroom because, look . . .

Yumma Yum Bird

. . . The endangered Yumma Yum Bird has made it's nest in my pile of dirty clothes. Trust me, you don't want to mess with one of them!!! (For proof, read my book 'The Grotty Spoon').

BONUS: SOCK CARPET EXCUSE

I was bored of my old carpet . . .

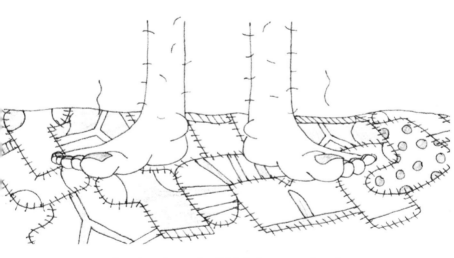

. . . So, instead of tidying my bedroom I've made a new carpet from all of the socks in my sock drawer (and also your sock drawer).

BONUS: HIDE AND SEEK EXCUSE

Shhhhhhhhhhhhhhhhhhh! . . .

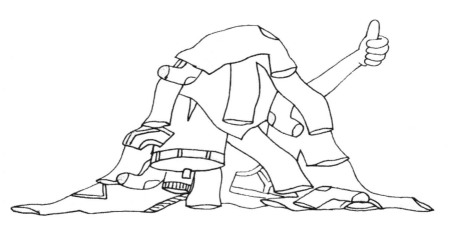

. . . I'm in the finals of the Hide and Seek World Championships. I can't tidy my bedroom as this is my world-class hiding place. Wish me luck!

BONUS: SOCK CIRCLES EXCUSE

Don't. Move. Anything! . . .

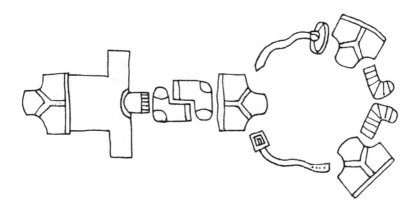

    . . . Aliens have left us an important message, and they've done so using my dirty laundry on the floor of my bedroom. We shall call it a 'sock circle'.

BONUS: CHORE OF NATURE EXCUSE

As 'the child', it is my chore-of-nature to create mess . . .

CHILDREN OF THE WORLD

THE DESTROYERS OF PEACE

. . . And as 'the parent', it is your chore-of-nature to tidy up. This is the circle of life that <u>MUST</u> be followed.

BONUS: WILD WEST EXCUSE

I can't tidy my bedroom . . .

. . . The Sheriff has finally cornered Billy the Kid in this Wild West Saloon for a daring shootout (due to commence in ten days time).

BONUS: THEIR MESS EXCUSE

But I've tidied up MY mess . . .

Little Sisters iPad

Big Brothers Mess

Ferguson the Cat's Toy

. . . You need to find the owners of this mess and get them to tidy it up.

BONUS: SOCK DRAWER DRAMA EXCUSE

I'll tidy my bedroom once I've caught up with my sock drawer drama . . .

Ted is mourning the sudden disappearance of Julie (who has actually run away with Pablo to start a new life in Spain

Sally returned from the airing cupboard and has been reunited with Bob

Jeff left Mindy for Cindy

. . . As you can see, there is A LOT to gossip about today.

BONUS: ONLINE COURSE EXCUSE

I want to make sure I do the best job possible . . .

. . . To tidy my bedroom properly, first I must learn how. That's why I've just enrolled on a ten week intensive online course.

ABOUT THE AUTHOR

James Warwood is (usually) very good at writing about himself. So he would like to start by saying that this bio was written on an off day.

He lives on the Welsh Border with his wife, two boys, and carnivorous plant. For some unknown reason he chose a career in Customer Service, mainly because it was indoor work and involves no manual labour. He writes and illustrates children's books by night like a superhero.

Anyway, people don't really read these bios, do they? They want to get on with reading a brand new book or play outside, not wade through paragraphs of text that attempts to make the author sound like a really interesting and accomplished person. Erm . . . drat, I've lost my rhythm.

WHERE TO FIND JAMES ONLINE

Website: www.cjwarwood.com
Goodreads: James Warwood
Instagram: CJWarwood
Twitter: @cjwarwood
Facebook: James Warwood

SO, WHAT'S NEXT?

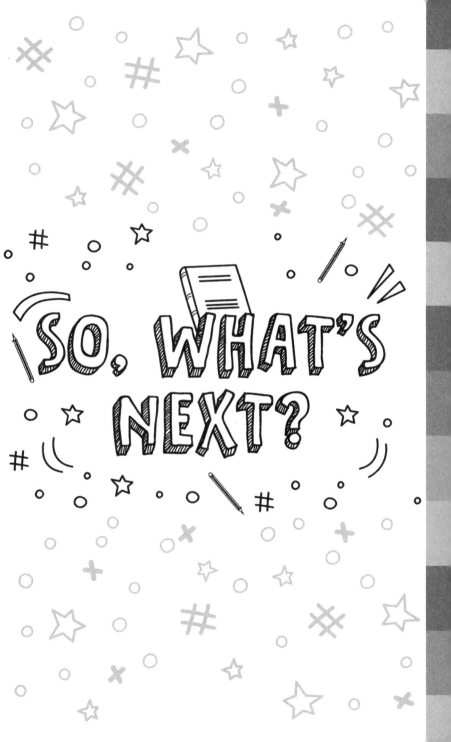

MIDDLE-GRADE STAND-ALONE FICTION

The Chef Who Cooked Up a Catastrophe
The Boy Who Stole One Million Socks
The Girl Who Vanquished the Dragon

TRUTH OR POOP?

True or false quiz books. Learn something new and laugh as you do it!

Book One: Amazing Animal Facts
Book Two: Spectacular Space Facts
Book Three: Gloriously Gross Facts

THE EXCUSE ENCYCLOPEDIA
Eleven more books to read!

Book 1 - 49 Excuses for Not Tidying Your Bedroom
Book 2 - 49 Ways to Steal the Cookie Jar
Book 3 - 49 Excuses for Not Doing Your Homework
Book 4 - 49 Questions to Annoy Your Parents
Book 5 - 49 Excuses for Skipping Gym Class
Book 6 - 49 Excuses for Staying Up Past Your Bedtime
Book 7 - 49 Excuses for Being Really Late
Book 8 - 49 Excuses For Not Eating Your Vegetables
Book 9 - 49 Excuses for Not Doing Your Chores
Book 10 - 49 Excuses for Getting the Most Out of
          Christmas
Book 11 - 49 Excuses for Extending Your Summer
          Holidays
Book 12 - 49 Excuses for Baggin More Candy at
          Halloween

Or get all 12 titles in 1 MASSIVE book!

The Excuse Encyclopedia: Books 1 - 12

Printed in Great Britain
by Amazon